Garter Snakes

Garter
Snakes

Mary Ann McDonald

THE CHILD'S WORLD®, INC.

Library of Congress Cataloging-in-Publication Data
McDonald, Mary Ann.
Garter snakes / by Mary Ann McDonald.
p.   cm.
Includes index.
Summary: Describes the physical characteristics,
behavior, habitat, and life cycle of this common reptile.
ISBN 1-56766-500-4 (lib. reinforced : alk paper)
1. Garter snakes—Juvenile literature.
[1. Garter snakes. 2. Snakes.]   I. Title.
QL666.O636M39   1998
597.96—dc21   97-40607
CIP
AC

Photo Credits

© 1993 A. B. Sheldon/Dembinsky Photo Assoc. Inc: 29
© 1997 Dick Scott/Dembinsky Photo Assoc. Inc: 9
© Francois Gohier, The National Audubon Society Collection/PR: 10
© 1997 Gary Meszaros/Dembinsky Photo Assoc. Inc: 6
© Jeff Lepore, The National Audubon Society Collection/PR: 15
© Joe McDonald: cover, 2, 13, 16, 20, 23, 29
© Robert and Linda Mitchell: 19, 24, 30

On the cover...

Front cover: This *blue striped garter snake* is looking for something to eat.
Page 2: This *eastern garter snake* is a very good swimmer.

Table of Contents

It is a sunny summer day, and you are in your garden, weeding tomatoes. Suddenly you hear a rustling under some nearby leaves. You move closer to see what is making the noise. The rustling gets louder. You move closer still, and a little striped snake slides out of the leaves and slithers away. What could this snake be? It's a garter snake!

⇐ This *Butler's garter snake* is watching its surroundings.

Where Do Garter Snakes Live?

Garter snakes are the most common snakes in North America. They live as far north as the Canadian Arctic and as far south as Mexico. They live along marshy coastlines, high up in the mountains, and in city parks and people's yards. About the only place they don't live is in the desert.

This eastern garter snake is exploring in the tall grass. ⇒

Garter snakes live under logs, rocks, or bushes or in other places where they can hide from enemies. During the cold winter months, they stay in holes in the ground called **dens**. Thousands of garter snakes might use the same den at one time.

What Do Garter Snakes Look Like?

Garter snakes have long, skinny bodies covered with scales. They can be brown, tan, olive, or black in color. Many have yellow or orange stripes, too. Some garter snakes are even white with pink eyes. These white garter snakes are called *albinos* (al-BY-noz). Albino snakes have short lives in the wild because they cannot hide from enemies.

Albino garter snakes like this one have trouble hiding. ⇒

A garter snake's skin is different from yours. As you grow, your skin grows too. But a garter snake's skin always stays the same size. As the snake gets bigger, it must lose its old skin and grow a bigger, newer one. The old skin dries up and peels off as the snake rubs against rocks and sticks. Losing the old skin is called **shedding**.

This eastern garter snake is shedding its old skin. ⇒

How Are Baby Garter Snakes Born?

After a male and female garter snake mate, several babies begin to grow inside the mother. They stay safe and warm inside clear, soft eggs. When the time is right, the mother pushes the eggs out of her body. Then the babies wriggle out of their eggs. Unlike many other animals, garter snake mothers do not help their babies. Newborn garter snakes must hunt and protect themselves right from the start.

⇐ This newborn garter snake is trying to wriggle out of its egg.

What Do Garter Snakes Eat?

Garter snakes are **carnivores**, which means that they eat other animals. Baby garter snakes eat slugs and earthworms. Adults eat frogs, salamanders, small birds, and mice. Some snakes have a poison, called **venom**, in their bite that helps kill their dinner. Garter snakes have no venom. Instead, they must grab their dinner, hold onto it, and eat it all at the same time! Garter snakes can be very helpful. That is because some of the animals they eat are garden pests.

This *Mexican garter snake* has just caught a tasty frog to eat. ⇒

How Do Garter Snakes Hunt?

Garter snakes hunt by watching for movement. They are nearsighted and cannot see anything more than about 15 inches away. If a frog stays very still, a garter snake might crawl right past it without ever seeing it. But if the frog moves, it becomes the snake's supper!

Garter snakes also use their tongues to "smell" where animals are hiding. The snake constantly flicks its tongue in and out of its mouth. The tongue picks up tiny pieces of dust from the air and ground. Special organs in the snake's mouth taste the dust. The snake uses this information to find food, other snakes, or the trail back to its den.

⇐ This blue striped garter snake is "smelling" with its tongue.

How Do Garter Snakes Move?

Garter snakes have different ways of moving on different kinds of surfaces. The most common way they move is by wiggling their bodies from side to side, looking for rough surfaces. They use these rough spots to push themselves forward. They use the same side-to-side motion for swimming, too. But what happens if a snake finds itself on a smooth floor without any rough surfaces? The snake just wiggles back and forth, unable to go anywhere.

This eastern garter snake is moving about on a log. ⇒

Do Garter Snakes Have Any Enemies?

Garter snakes have many enemies. Baby garter snakes look just like worms, and birds, frogs, turtles, and even other snakes like to eat them. Adult garter snakes are eaten by hawks, raccoons, foxes, and even bobcats.

Garter snakes protect themselves by crawling away or hiding under things. Their coloring helps them blend in with nearby grass and leaves. Coloring that helps an animal hide is called **camouflage**.

⇐ This *checkered garter snake* is hiding in some leaves.

How Do Garter Snakes Stay Safe?

If a garter snake does get caught, it gives off a stinky, greasy oil called **musk**. Musk not only smells bad, many animals think it tastes bad, too. A fox or bird might think the smelly snake is dead and let it go. If you pick up a wild garter snake, you might get musked, too.

Are Garter Snakes in Danger?

Garter snakes live in many different types of places, so most of them are in little danger of dying out. But one type, the *San Francisco garter snake*, has almost died out. Building around the city of San Francisco has destroyed many areas where this snake lives. People are trying to protect some places where the snakes can live, but no one knows whether this effort will be in time.

San Francisco garter snakes like this one are becoming very rare. ⇒

How Can You Study Garter Snakes?

Because garter snakes live in so many different places, you might be able to find one where you live. Once you find it, try watching it for several days. Where does it lie in the sun? What time of day do you see it?

Sit very still near the snake and just watch it quietly. If you don't move, you won't scare or harm it. If you are patient enough, you might even see the snake hunt and catch its food! There is plenty to learn about these fascinating animals.

⇐ This Mexican garter snake is curling up for a nap.

Glossary

camouflage (KAM–uh–flazh)
Camouflage is coloring that makes an animal hard to see. A garter snake's coloring blends in with the grasses and leaves around it.

carnivores (KAR–nih–vorz)
Carnivores are animals that eat other animals. Garter snakes are carnivores.

dens (DENZ)
Dens are cozy hollows that animals call home. During the winter, garter snakes live in underground dens.

musk (MUSK)
Musk is a smelly, greasy oil some animals produce. Garter snakes produce musk to help them escape danger.

shedding (SHED–ding)
Shedding is getting rid of an old, outgrown skin. Garter snakes shed their skin many times.

venom (VEN–num)
Venom is poison that some snakes use to kill their food. Garter snakes have no venom in their bites.

Index